Ben and Paul

Alex Lane
Illustrated by Deborah Allwright

OXFORD

This is Ben.
Ben is tall.

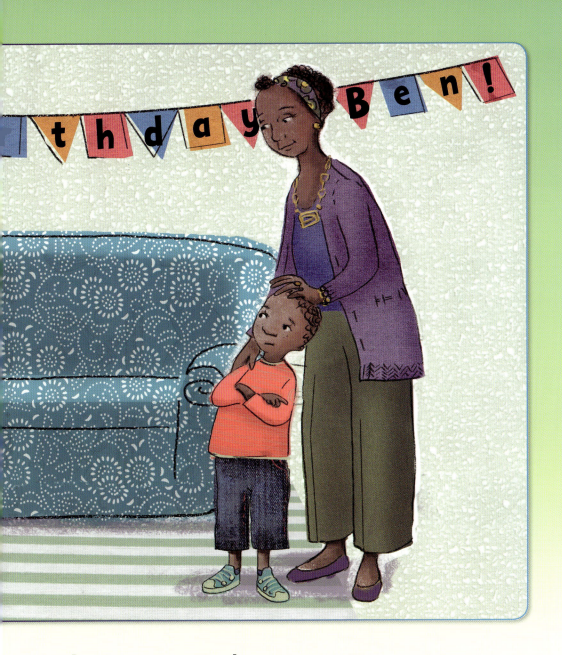

This is Paul.
Paul is small.

Dad gives Ben a present.
What can it be?

Paul looks sad.
He is small.

Mum gives Ben a present.
What can it be?

Paul looks sad.
He is small.

Gran gives Ben a present.
What can it be?

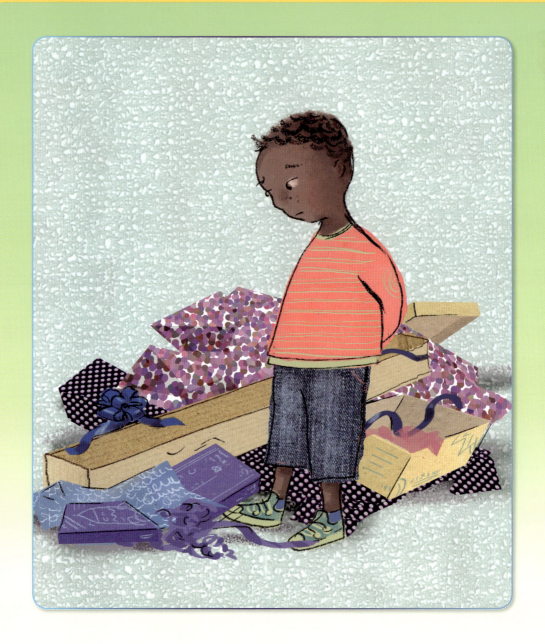

Paul looks sad.
He is small.

13

Paul gives Ben a present.
It is small. But ...

... it is the best present of all!